ILLINOIS TEST PREP
Writing Skills Workbook
IAR Guided Practice
Grade 7

© 2019 by L. Hawas

All rights reserved. No part of this book may be reproduced or transmitted in any form or by any means, electronic, mechanical, photocopying, recording, or otherwise without prior written permission.

ISBN 978-1795252911

TEST MASTER PRESS

www.testmasterpress.com

Writing Skills Workbook, IAR Guided Practice, Grade 7

CONTENTS

Introduction	4
Reading and Writing Practice Set 1	5
Short Passages, Long Passage with Essay, Personal Narrative Writing Task	
Reading and Writing Practice Set 2	17
Short Passages, Short Story Writing Task, Argument Writing Task	
Reading and Writing Practice Set 3	27
Short Passages, Long Passage with Essay, Explanatory Writing Task	
Reading and Writing Practice Set 4	41
Short Passages, Argument Writing Task, Short Story Writing Task	
Reading and Writing Practice Set 5	51
Short Passages, Long Passage with Essay, Explanatory Writing Task	
Reading and Writing Practice Set 6	65
Short Passages, Short Story Writing Task, Argument Writing Task	
Reading and Writing Practice Set 7	75
Short Passages, Long Passage with Essay, Explanatory Writing Task	
Reading and Writing Practice Set 8	87
Short Passages, Argument Writing Task, Short Story Writing Task	
Reading and Writing Practice Set 9	99
Short Passages, Long Passage with Essay, Personal Narrative Writing Task	
Reading and Writing Practice Set 10	111
Short Passages, Short Story Writing Task, Argument Writing Task	
Answer Key	123
Informational/Explanatory Writing Rubric	134
Argument Writing Rubric	135
Narrative Writing Rubric	136

INTRODUCTION
For Parents, Teachers, and Tutors

Developing Reading and Writing Skills

The state of Illinois has adopted the Illinois Learning Standards. These standards describe what students are expected to know. Students will be instructed based on these standards and the Illinois Assessment of Readiness (IAR) tests will include questions based on these standards. This workbook will develop the reading and writing skills that students are expected to have, while preparing students for the state tests and giving students practice completing a range of reading and writing tasks. The emphasis in this workbook is on writing skills, but complementary reading skills are also covered as students complete tasks involving providing written answers to reading comprehension questions.

Completing Practice Sets

This workbook is divided into 10 practice sets. Each practice set includes four tasks that progress from simple to more complex. The types of tasks are described below.

Task Type	Details
Short Passage with Questions	These tasks contain a short passage followed by reading comprehension questions requiring written answers. They also include a Core Writing Skills Practice exercise that focuses on one key writing skill. These exercises may require students to respond to a text, complete a research project, or complete a writing task.
Long Passage with Essay Question	These tasks contain a long passage followed by an essay question requiring a written answer of 1 to 2 pages. They also include hints and planning guidance to help students develop effective writing skills.
Personal Narrative Writing Task	These tasks contain a writing prompt for a personal narrative, as well as hints and planning guidance.
Short Story Writing Task	These tasks contain a writing prompt for a story, as well as hints and planning guidance.
Argument Writing Task	These tasks contain a writing prompt for an argument, as well as hints and planning guidance.
Explanatory Writing Task	These tasks contain a writing prompt for an essay, as well as hints and planning guidance.

By completing the practice sets, students will have experience with all types of writing tasks. This includes writing in response to passages, writing all the types of texts covered in the Illinois Learning Standards, gathering information from sources, and completing research projects.

Some of the writing tasks also include guides for editing and revising completed work. This encourages students to review their work and improve on it, while the checklists help ensure that students focus on the key criteria that work is judged on. This will help prepare students for the writing tasks found on assessments, as well as guide students on the key features of strong student writing.

Preparing for the Illinois Assessment of Readiness

In 2019, students in Illinois will take a new test instead of the previously used PARCC assessments. The new test is the Illinois Assessment of Readiness, or IAR. This book will help prepare students for the IAR tests. Strong writing skills are essential for performing well on the new tests. The assessments include reading comprehension questions requiring written answers as well as writing tasks where students write essays and narratives. In addition, students need to be able to read texts closely and analyze and evaluate texts.

The questions and exercises will develop the more advanced reading skills needed, provide extensive experience providing written answers, and help students learn to write effective essays and narratives. This will ensure that students have the skills and experience they need to perform well on the assessments.

Reading and Writing Practice Set 1

This practice set contains four writing tasks. These are described below.

Task 1: Short Passage with Questions

This task has a short passage followed by questions. Read each question carefully. Then write your answer in the space provided.

You can also practice writing skills by completing the Core Writing Skills Practice exercise.

Task 2: Short Passage with Questions

This task has a short passage followed by questions. Read each question carefully. Then write your answer in the space provided.

You can also practice writing skills by completing the Core Writing Skills Practice exercise.

Task 3: Long Passage with Essay Question

This task has a longer passage with an essay question. Read the passage, complete the planning page, and then write or type your answer.

Task 4: Personal Narrative Writing Task

This final task requires you to write a personal narrative. Read the writing prompt, complete the planning page, and then write or type your answer.

Task 1: Short Passage with Questions

The Dog and the River

A dog was crossing a river by walking across a log. He had a small but juicy piece of meat in his mouth. He walked slowly across the log, while being careful not to lose his balance. As he looked down, he saw his own reflection in the water. He mistook the reflection for another dog. As he stared at the dog, he realized that the piece of meat it was carrying was larger than his own. He immediately dropped his own piece of meat and attacked the other dog to get the larger piece.

As he barked at the dog, his piece of meat fell from his mouth and into the water below. His paw struck at his reflection, only to hit the water below. At that moment, he realized that the other dog was only his reflection. He stared sadly at his small piece of meat as it floated away.

CORE WRITING SKILLS PRACTICE

Think about the lesson the dog learns in the passage. Describe **one** way you could apply this lesson to your own life.

_____

_____

_____

_____

_____

_____

1 What genre is the passage? Explain your answer.

Hint — Genre refers to the category a work of literature falls into. Identify the genre and then describe one or two features of the passage that show what genre it is.

_____

_____

_____

_____

2 How does the imagery at the end of the passage reveal the dog's feelings?

Hint — Focus on how the author describes the dog after he drops the meat. Describe what his actions suggest about how he feels.

_____

_____

_____

_____

_____

Task 2: Short Passage with Questions

Understanding Genius

Did you know that the remains of Einstein's brain are stored at Princeton Hospital in New Jersey? Dr. Thomas Harvey was the doctor who had to conduct the initial autopsy on Einstein in 1955. Harvey removed Einstein's brain without permission from Einstein's family. He carefully sliced it into sections to keep for research. It was an unethical thing to do, but it has provided valuable information to scientists. It remains controversial to this day. There are some who argue that it should never have been done. There are others who believe that the information that could potentially be gained was worth it.

There are now at least three published papers relating to the study of Einstein's brain. Scientists have attempted to understand what made Einstein a genius, and have determined that his brain did have some unique features. One part of the brain called the parietal lobe was larger than normal. It was also not separated into two compartments, as it is in normal brains. This could help explain Einstein's intelligence, creativity, and mathematical ability.

CORE WRITING SKILLS PRACTICE

The author states that studying Einstein's brain "has provided valuable information to scientists." How does the author support this claim?

_____

_____

_____

_____

_____

1. Explain why "Understanding Genius" is a suitable title for the passage.

   Hint: To answer this question, explain how this title relates to the main idea of the passage.

   _____
   _____
   _____
   _____

2. Do you agree or disagree with Dr. Thomas Harvey's actions?

   Hint: This question is asking for your personal opinion. You may agree or you may disagree. However, be sure to describe why you have that opinion.

   _____
   _____
   _____
   _____

Task 3: Long Passage with Essay Question

Directions: Read the passage below. Then answer the question that follows. Use the planning page to plan your writing. Then write or type your essay.

The Loch Ness Monster

The Loch Ness Monster is a creature that is reported to inhabit Loch Ness, a lake in the Scottish Highlands. Its existence has never been proven despite several thousands of reported sightings since 1930. Any examples of photographic evidence or sonar readings that have been offered have been disputed by experts. Modern scientists believe the Loch Ness Monster to be a myth. They claim that any sightings are either deliberate hoaxes or the results of wishful thinking. Another school of thought suggests that the Loch Ness Monster does exist and is in fact a survivor of the dinosaur age.

This theory also applies to similar creatures that have been sighted in other Scottish lakes. It suggests that the Loch Ness Monster is part of the long-surviving plesiosaurs family. These were carnivorous breeds of reptile that first emerged during the Triassic period. Their physical appearance fits the typical description of the Loch Ness Monster and also many of the images captured by camera. Despite this, scientists claim that the plesiosaurs family became extinct thousands of years ago. Many consider the Loch Ness Monster to be little more than a complete fabrication.

Believers considered that a breakthrough had been made in 2007. At this time, a lab technician named Gordon Holmes captured a detailed video of what he described to be the Loch Ness Monster. He claimed to have filmed a 14-meter long creature moving quickly beneath the surface of the water. He submitted the tape to a marine biologist at the Loch Ness 2000 center. After an initial review, it was described as the best footage that had been recorded since the turn of the century. Many considered that it may offer final proof of the existence of the Loch Ness Monster.

Further inspection of the tape raised some serious concerns. It was thought that the creature captured on film was likely to be a sea otter or water bird. Gordon Holmes himself then became the subject of discussion and was dismissed as someone who either faked or exaggerated the footage. He was known to have a long history of sighting mythical creatures and fairies. This mistrust of the evidence suggests that even modern technology will be unable to confirm whether the Loch Ness Monster is a real creature.

Various expeditions have been led to search for the monster since 1962. The most recent of these was carried out by the BBC in 2003. In this study, 600 separate solar beams and satellites were used to track any motion in the water. Despite the advanced technology, no large or unusual animal was detected throughout the search. It is believed that the failure of this expedition is the final proof that the Loch Ness Monster is only a myth.

© Sam Fentress, Wikimedia Commons

1   Do you think that the Loch Ness Monster is real or just a myth? Use details from the passage to support your answer.

In your answer, be sure to
- give your opinion on whether you think the Loch Ness Monster is real or a myth
- use details from the passage to support your answer
- write an answer of between 1 and 2 pages

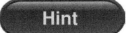

This question is asking you to form an opinion based on the passage. You can decide either way. However, be sure to come up with reasonable explanations of why you have that opinion.

You should mainly refer to the details given in the passage to support your opinion. However, you can also include ideas of your own that expand on the information. For example, the passage states that there have been reported sightings since 1930. You could use this detail to argue that if the Loch Ness Monster was real, there would be some proof of it by now.

Planning Page

Summary
Write a brief summary of what you are going to write about.

Supporting Details
Write down the facts, details, or examples you are going to include in your answer.

Outline
Write a plan for what you are going to write. Include the main points you want to cover and the order you will cover them.

Task 4: Personal Narrative Writing Task

Directions: Read the writing prompt below. Use the planning page to plan your writing. Then write or type your answer.

They say that you should not judge a book by its cover. But people often make quick judgments about people that turn out to be wrong. Think about a time when you judged someone too quickly. Who did you judge and what judgment did you make?

Write a composition describing a time when you judged someone too quickly. Describe who you judged, what judgment you made, and how you learned that your judgment was wrong.

Hint

Make sure you answer each part of the question. Remember that you need to include the following:
- who you judged
- what judgment you made about the person
- what happened to make you realize that your judgment was wrong

When you write your outline, make sure that it covers all of the parts of the question.

Planning Page

Summary

Write a brief summary of what you are going to write about.

Outline

Write a plan for what you are going to write. Include the main points you want to cover and the order you will cover them.

Writing and Editing Checklist

After you finish writing your personal narrative, you can use this guide to review and edit your work. Use the questions as a guide to finding ways you can improve your work.

Writing Checklist

- ✓ Does your work have a strong opening? Does it introduce the main ideas or set the scene well?
- ✓ Is your work well-organized? Is related information grouped together? Does each paragraph have one main idea?
- ✓ Does your work have an effective ending? Does it tie up the events well?
- ✓ Is your work focused? Are there any details that do not fit with your main ideas?
- ✓ Do your ideas flow well? Have you used words and phrases to link ideas well?
- ✓ Have you used strong words? Are there words that could be replaced with better ones?
- ✓ Have you used effective descriptions? Could your descriptions be improved?
- ✓ Have you used sensory details? Could you add more sensory details to help readers imagine the scene?

Editing Checklist

- ✓ Have you used a variety of sentence structures? Are your sentences all written correctly?
- ✓ Is the grammar correct?
- ✓ Are all words spelled correctly? You can check the spelling of any words you are not sure of.
- ✓ Is punctuation used correctly?
- ✓ If dialogue is used, is it punctuated correctly?
- ✓ Are all words capitalized correctly?

Reading and Writing

Practice Set 2

This practice set contains four writing tasks. These are described below.

Task 1: Short Passage with Questions

This task has a short passage followed by questions. Read each question carefully. Then write your answer in the space provided.

You can also practice writing skills by completing the Core Writing Skills Practice exercise.

Task 2: Short Passage with Questions

This task has a short passage followed by questions. Read each question carefully. Then write your answer in the space provided.

You can also practice writing skills by completing the Core Writing Skills Practice exercise.

Task 3: Short Story Writing Task

This task requires you to write a short story. Read the writing prompt, complete the planning page, and then write or type your answer.

Task 4: Argument Writing Task

This final task requires you to write an argument. Read the writing prompt, complete the planning page, and then write or type your answer.

Task 1: Short Passage with Questions

Bananas

Dear Diary,

Today Dad told me that I've been opening a banana wrong all of my life. I thought he was messing with me!

Then Dad took me to the zoo and showed me how a monkey opens a banana. They don't do it from the stem end. They grab the tip, pinch it, and peel one side down, and then peel the other side. It's so easy. I have to admit I was impressed.

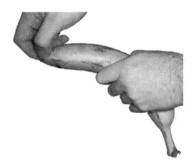

Well, now I know I've been opening a banana wrong all of my life. I don't know what is worse – having to admit that Dad was right or having to admit that a monkey is smarter than me!

Bye for now,

Harmanie

CORE WRITING SKILLS PRACTICE

In the passage, Harmanie describes how monkeys open bananas. Imagine that you want to teach people how to open a banana this way. Write a set of instructions describing how to open a banana.

Step 1. _____

Step 2. _____

Step 3. _____

Step 4. _____

1   Explain what the phrase "messing with me" means.

_____
_____
_____
_____
_____

2   How is the way Harmanie opens bananas different from how monkeys open bananas?

Hint This question is asking you to summarize specific information given in the passage. Make sure you use your own words when writing your answer.

_____
_____
_____
_____
_____

Task 2: Short Passage with Questions

Antique Map

It's really easy and fun to make a map look like it's an old antique. You'll need to print out a map or get permission to use an old map that is no longer needed. You'll also need to make some strong black tea (make sure you let it cool down) and a spray bottle to put the tea in.

Step 1: Cover a desk or table with plastic wrap or a plastic sheet so you don't damage the desk or table. Place the map on the plastic.

Step 2: Soak the entire map by spraying it evenly with black tea.

Step 3: Gently lift the map after it is sprayed to make sure it does not stick to the flat surface.

Step 4: Allow the map to dry and repeat steps 1 to 3 until you achieve the desired effect.

Step 5: Add some marks and tears to the edges of map.

CORE WRITING SKILLS PRACTICE

Instructions often include a list of items that are needed. Write a list of items needed that could be added to the passage.

1. _____

2. _____

3. _____

4. _____

1 Why does the author say to repeat steps 1 to 3? What would happen each time the steps were repeated?

_____

_____

_____

_____

2 Why do you think it is important to let the tea cool down?

Hint — This question asks you the reason for a specific direction in the passage. Use your own knowledge to work out why it would be important to let the tea cool down.

_____

_____

_____

_____

Task 3: Short Story Writing Task

Directions: Read the writing prompt below. Use the planning page to plan your writing. Then write or type your answer.

Marina had always dreamed of sailing around the world. She wanted to discover a new island that nobody had ever been to before.

Write a story about Marina's journey and the place she discovered.

Hint

The writing prompt tells you that your story should be about Marina's journey. Use this as the starting point and think of a story based around this idea. Remember that a story should have a main problem that is solved by the end of it. The main problem in this story could be that Marina cannot find a new island, or it could be something that happens once she finds the new island. Focus your story around the main problem you select.

Start by introducing the main problem at the start of the story. Then describe how Marina tries to solve it. End with a conclusion that solves the problem and ties up the story. By approaching the writing task this way, you will end up with a focused story that is well-organized and flows well.

Planning Page

The Story
Write a summary of your story.

The Beginning
Describe what is going to happen at the start of your story.

The Middle
Describe what is going to happen in the middle of your story.

The End
Describe what is going to happen at the end of your story.

Task 4: Argument Writing Task

Directions: Read the writing prompt below. Use the planning page to plan your writing. Then write or type your answer.

Your school is planning to start a program to encourage recycling. The school will recycle paper, bottles, and aluminum cans. All students will have to help with the recycling program for at least 2 hours per week. There has been some debate about the program. Some people believe that it is worthwhile and will be good for students, while others believe that the school should focus on teaching students.

Write a letter to your school principal expressing your opinion on whether or not the program should go ahead. Use reasons, facts, and/or examples to support your opinion.

Hint

The writing prompt describes the purpose of your writing. In this case, you want to give your opinion on whether or not the program should go ahead. Make sure you first decide whether you will argue that the program should go ahead, or that the program should not go ahead. Then you will need to give reasons to support your opinion. Think of two or three good reasons to use in your letter.

Planning Page

Summary
Write a brief summary of your claim.

Supporting Details
Write down the facts, details, or examples you are going to include.

Outline
Write a plan for what you are going to write. Include the main points you want to cover and the order you will cover them.

Writing and Editing Checklist

After you finish writing your argument, you can use this guide to review and edit your work. Use the questions as a guide to finding ways you can improve your work.

Writing Checklist

- ✓ Does your work have one clear claim?
- ✓ Does your work have a strong opening? Does the opening introduce the topic and state the claim?
- ✓ Is your claim supported? Have you used clear reasons to support your claim?
- ✓ Have you used enough evidence? Is your evidence all relevant?
- ✓ Is your work well-organized? Is related information grouped together? Does each paragraph have one main idea?
- ✓ Do your ideas flow well? Have you used words and phrases to link ideas well?
- ✓ Does your work have a strong ending? Does the ending restate the main idea and tie up the argument?

Editing Checklist

- ✓ Have you used a variety of sentence structures? Are your sentences all written correctly?
- ✓ Is the grammar correct?
- ✓ Are all words spelled correctly? You can check the spelling of any words you are not sure of.
- ✓ Is punctuation used correctly?
- ✓ Are all words capitalized correctly?

Writing Skills Workbook, IAR Guided Practice, Grade 7

Reading and Writing

Practice Set 3

This practice set contains four writing tasks. These are described below.

Task 1: Short Passage with Questions

This task has a short passage followed by questions. Read each question carefully. Then write your answer in the space provided.

You can also practice writing skills by completing the Core Writing Skills Practice exercise.

Task 2: Short Passage with Questions

This task has a short passage followed by questions. Read each question carefully. Then write your answer in the space provided.

You can also practice writing skills by completing the Core Writing Skills Practice exercise.

Task 3: Long Passage with Essay Question

This task has a longer passage with an essay question. Read the passage, complete the planning page, and then write or type your answer.

Task 4: Explanatory Writing Task

This final task requires you to write an essay that explains something. Read the writing prompt, complete the planning page, and then write or type your answer.

Task 1: Short Passage with Questions

Photosynthesis

The process of turning light energy into chemical energy is called photosynthesis. The process of photosynthesis is how plants get their energy.

Plant leaves and stems have a high amount of a green pigment named chlorophyll contained in them. Light energy from the Sun is absorbed by the chlorophyll. This energy is used to power a reaction between water and carbon dioxide. This reaction produces glucose and oxygen. The plant stores the glucose and uses it for energy. The oxygen is released into the air.

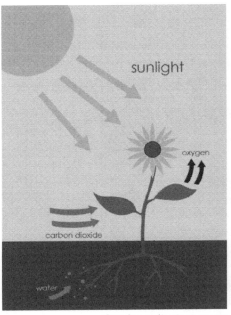

©Wikimedia Commons

CORE WRITING SKILLS PRACTICE

The word *photosynthesis* contains the Greek root *photo*, which means light, and the word *synthesis*, which refers to combining elements in a chemical reaction. The word *photosynthesis* refers to using light to combine elements. Use the word parts of the following words to guess their technical meanings.

chronometer _____

biohazard _____

polychrome _____

hydrophobia _____

1   Define the term *photosynthesis*.

Hint The passage tells you the meaning of the term. Write your own definition by paraphrasing the information in the passage.

_____

_____

_____

_____

2   Complete the diagram by describing the main steps of photosynthesis in sequence.

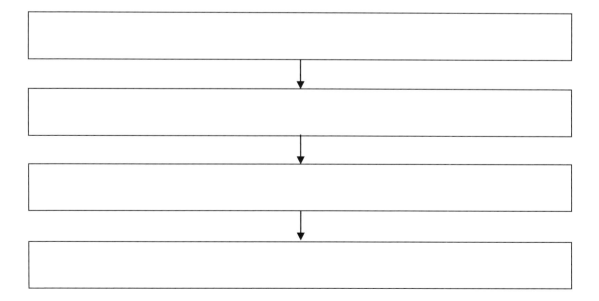

Task 2: Short Passage with Questions

A Special Student

June enjoyed being in school. She liked watching the children play and sometimes sharing their lunches. She liked seeing her friends play skip rope and having a nap in the afternoons. June sometimes enjoyed eating the grass on the football field. June wasn't an ordinary student. She was the school mascot.

Every week, June would enjoy having a class of children milk her. Then she would be let out into the paddock for a graze. If it was warm outside, June would stay in the shelter of a tree or stay in her barn. What June liked best of all, is when the children petted her. There were always plenty of children happy to pat her, so June was a very happy school mascot. The children loved June just as much as she loved them. They enjoyed spending time with her and looking after her.

CORE WRITING SKILLS PRACTICE
WRITE A SHORT STORY

Think of something interesting that could happen to June. Use your imagination and think of an exciting or unusual event. She might go missing, or she might even learn how to talk. Write a short description below of what happens to June. Then write a complete short story describing the event.

_____

_____

_____

_____

_____

_____

1 Why do you think the author does not reveal that June is a cow in the first paragraph?

Hint To answer this question, you have to think about the author's purpose. Focus on what influence this has on the reader.

_____

_____

_____

_____

2 Complete the chart below using details from the passage.

Details that Show that June is a Cow

1)
2)
3)

3 Do you think that June is looked after well? Explain why or why not.

Hint You should use the information given in the passage to form your opinion. In your answer, use two or three details about June to support your answer.

Writing and Editing Checklist

After you finish writing your answer to question 3, you can use this guide to review and edit your work. Use the questions as a guide to finding ways you can improve your work.

Writing Checklist

- ✓ Does your work have one clear claim?
- ✓ Does your work have a strong opening? Does the opening introduce the topic and state the claim?
- ✓ Is your claim supported? Have you used clear reasons to support your claim?
- ✓ Have you used enough evidence? Is your evidence all relevant?
- ✓ Is your work well-organized? Is related information grouped together? Does each paragraph have one main idea?
- ✓ Do your ideas flow well? Have you used words and phrases to link ideas well?
- ✓ Does your work have a strong ending? Does the ending restate the main idea and tie up the argument?

Editing Checklist

- ✓ Have you used a variety of sentence structures? Are your sentences all written correctly?
- ✓ Is the grammar correct?
- ✓ Are all words spelled correctly? You can check the spelling of any words you are not sure of.
- ✓ Is punctuation used correctly?
- ✓ Are all words capitalized correctly?

Task 3: Long Passage with Essay Question

Directions: Read the passage below. Then answer the question that follows. Use the planning page to plan your writing. Then write or type your essay.

Sir Isaac Newton

Sir Isaac Newton was an English born physicist and mathematician. He also had a keen interest in astronomy, philosophy, alchemy, and theology. He was born on January 4, 1643 and died on March 31, 1727 at the age of 84. It was in the field of physics where Sir Isaac Newton carried out his best and most important work.

Newton is widely recognized as the first person to understand gravity. He also developed the three laws of motion. These laws became the foundations for scientists' work through the following centuries. Newton's work showed that the motion of objects is governed by a rigid set of natural laws. These laws applied to objects on the Earth as well as the planets themselves.

Sir Isaac Newton's thirst for knowledge was applied to all aspects of science. He studied the speed of sound, and designed the first reflecting telescope for practical use. He also developed an advanced theory of color. He even developed a universal law of cooling.

Newton's Laws of Motion

Newton's First Law of Motion	An object will remain at rest unless acted on by an unbalanced force.
Newton's Second Law of Motion	The acceleration of an object depends on its mass and the net force.
Newton's Third Law of Motion	For every action, there is an equal and opposite reaction.

Sir Isaac Newton's work in the field of mathematics was also groundbreaking. His studies are said to have advanced every mathematics theory in practice today. Credit for some of his findings is shared with a German philosopher called Gottfried Leibniz. The basis of their work was applied to developing fractions and equations as mathematical tools. His continued hard work in the field led to him being appointed a Professor of Mathematics in 1669.

Sir Isaac Newton was also a deeply religious man. It is a little-known fact that he wrote more papers on religion than he did on physics and mathematics. Many of his religious papers were ahead of their time. They were opposed to many beliefs held in the 17th century.

Sir Isaac Newton is widely considered to be one of the most influential men of all time. His work has inspired much of the scientific and mathematical knowledge that is widely used today. Despite this, Newton was a modest man who often praised the work of others who had gone before him. In 1999, a poll of modern experts revealed that Sir Isaac Newton was considered to be the greatest physicist of all time. He shared the title with Albert Einstein.

1. How does the author show that Sir Isaac Newton had a strong influence on science? Use details from the passage to support your answer.

   In your answer, be sure to
   - describe how the author shows that Sir Isaac Newton had a strong influence on science
   - use details from the passage in your answer
   - write an answer of between 1 and 2 pages

The passage includes many details that show the influence that Sir Isaac Newton had. To answer this question, you should focus on identifying all the examples that show Newton's influence. Then plan your answer based around these examples. However, be sure not to just list every example in the passage in the author's words. Instead, use your own words and write a well-organized essay that uses the examples in the passage.

Planning Page

Summary
Write a brief summary of what you are going to write about.

Supporting Details
Write down the facts, details, or examples you are going to include in your answer.

Outline
Write a plan for what you are going to write. Include the main points you want to cover and the order you will cover them.

Task 4: Explanatory Writing Task

Directions: Read the writing prompt below. Use the planning page to plan your writing. Then write or type your answer.

Parties are held for many reasons. There are birthday parties, farewell parties, and parties for holidays like Independence Day. Think of some parties that you have enjoyed. What made those parties enjoyable? Was it the people there, was it having good food, was it having fun things to do, or was it having something to celebrate together? Decide on two or three things that you think make a good party.

Write an essay describing what makes a party enjoyable. In your answer, identify two or three features that make a good party and explain why each feature is important.

Hint

The writing prompt tells you to identify two or three features of a good party. Use this as the basis of how you organize your essay.

You should start with a paragraph that introduces the topic of parties and what makes them enjoyable.

The body of your essay will then have one paragraph for each feature you identify. Start each of these paragraphs by stating the feature. Then explain why it is important and how it makes a party enjoyable. Use details and examples to support your ideas.

The final paragraph will conclude the essay by summing up your main ideas.

Planning Page

Summary

Write a brief summary of what you are going to write about.

Outline

Write a plan for what you are going to write. Include the main points you want to cover and the order you will cover them.

Writing and Editing Checklist

After you finish writing your essay, you can use this guide to review and edit your work. Use the questions as a guide to finding ways you can improve your work.

Writing Checklist

- ✓ Does your work have a strong opening? Does it introduce the topic and the main ideas?
- ✓ Is your work well-organized? Is related information grouped together? Does each paragraph have one main idea?
- ✓ Have you included facts, details, and examples to support your ideas?
- ✓ Is your work focused? Are there any details that do not fit with your main ideas?
- ✓ Do your ideas flow well? Have you used words and phrases to link ideas well?
- ✓ Does your work have a strong ending?

Editing Checklist

- ✓ Have you used a variety of sentence structures? Are your sentences all written correctly?
- ✓ Is the grammar correct?
- ✓ Are all words spelled correctly? You can check the spelling of any words you are not sure of.
- ✓ Is punctuation used correctly?
- ✓ Are all words capitalized correctly?

Writing Skills Workbook, IAR Guided Practice, Grade 7

Reading and Writing

Practice Set 4

This practice set contains four writing tasks. These are described below.

Task 1: Short Passage with Questions

This task has a short passage followed by questions. Read each question carefully. Then write your answer in the space provided.

You can also practice writing skills by completing the Core Writing Skills Practice exercise.

Task 2: Short Passage with Questions

This task has a short passage followed by questions. Read each question carefully. Then write your answer in the space provided.

You can also practice writing skills by completing the Core Writing Skills Practice exercise.

Task 3: Argument Writing Task

This task requires you to write an argument. Read the writing prompt, complete the planning page, and then write or type your answer.

Task 4: Short Story Writing Task

This task requires you to write a short story. Read the writing prompt, complete the planning page, and then write or type your answer.

Task 1: Short Passage with Questions

The Little Things

Every morning when Patrick woke up he would throw up his arms, let out a yawn, and jump out of bed.

"Up and at 'em," he'd always bellow loudly.

Patrick had his breakfast and then got dressed in his overalls. He strolled out to his garden to tend to his vibrant flowers and gourmet vegetable patch. Every afternoon, he would bring in new flowers for his wife and some fresh vegetables for dinner.

"It's the little things that make life great," Patrick would always say.

CORE WRITING SKILLS PRACTICE

Do you agree that the little things make life great? Explain why or why not.

_____

_____

_____

_____

_____

_____

_____

1   Describe the main theme of the passage.

   _____
   _____
   _____
   _____

2   How does the author create a joyous mood in the passage?

   Hint   Think about the way the author describes Patrick's actions and the words the author uses when giving details about Patrick's life.

   _____
   _____
   _____
   _____

Task 2: Short Passage with Questions

Sweet Tooth

Did you know that people originally used to chew sugarcane raw? Sugar has been produced since ancient times and originated in India. However, sugar wasn't always so plentiful or so inexpensive. In the early days, honey was used more often than sugar for sweetening food and beverages. At this time, people used to chew on sugarcane, where the sugar was in the form of sugarcane juice. Later, people learned how to turn sugarcane juice into crystallized sugar. This allowed sugar to be stored and transported. This new development was the beginning of sugar becoming more widespread.

At first, sugar remained expensive and was considered a luxury ingredient. Over time, sugarcane crops became more popular and more and more people had access to sugar. It became common to add sugar to foods. Sugar was also one of the first ingredients used, as it is today, to mask the bitter taste of medicine. Today, sugar is a standard ingredient in a whole range of products and most people have a store of sugar in the pantry.

CORE WRITING SKILLS PRACTICE

Describe how the second paragraph is mainly organized.

_____

_____

_____

_____

_____

1. Describe **three** ways that sugar use has changed over time.

   1: _____

   _____

   2: _____

   _____

   3: _____

   _____

2. Which development in sugar's history had the greatest impact on its use?

   Hint — This question is asking you to draw a conclusion from the passage. Support your conclusion by including details about the impact the development had.

   _____

   _____

   _____

   _____

   _____

   _____

Task 3: Argument Writing Task

Directions: Read the writing prompt below. Use the planning page to plan your writing. Then write or type your answer.

Read this piece of advice.

> It's not how good you are. It's how good you want to be.
> -Paul Arden

Do you think this is good advice? Explain why or why not.

Hint

Start by thinking about what the advice means. It means that you should focus more on what you want to achieve than what you can achieve right now. Then think about whether you agree. Think about how this advice relates to your life.

The advice can be applied to many areas. A good essay will be focused. Think about how it relates to one area of your life. It could be your studies, your sporting achievements, or a goal you have set for yourself. As you plan your writing, focus on this one area. This will help make sure you produce writing that has a clear and focused idea.

Planning Page

Summary

Write a brief summary of your claim.

Supporting Details

Write down the facts, details, or examples you are going to include.

Outline

Write a plan for what you are going to write. Include the main points you want to cover and the order you will cover them.

Task 4: Short Story Writing Task

Directions: Read the writing prompt below. Use the planning page to plan your writing. Then write or type your answer.

Maxwell had never won a prize before. Then the phone call came. He had won something so exciting that he could hardly believe it.

Write a story about Maxwell and the prize that he wins.

Hint

You can make your story more interesting by choosing a point of view that suits what the story is about. In this story, you will probably want readers to understand how excited Maxwell is. This would suit a first person point of view. By writing this story in a first person point of view as if you are Maxwell, you will be able to show Maxwell's thoughts, feelings, and emotions.

You can also use other tools in your story, such as by using dialogue. In this story, you could use dialogue to describe the phone call that Maxwell receives. This would be a good way to make your story seem real and to move the action along.

Planning Page

The Story
Write a summary of your story.

The Beginning
Describe what is going to happen at the start of your story.

The Middle
Describe what is going to happen in the middle of your story.

The End
Describe what is going to happen at the end of your story.

Writing and Editing Checklist

After you finish writing your story, you can use this guide to review and edit your work. Use the questions as a guide to finding ways you can improve your work.

Writing Checklist

- ✓ Does your story have a strong opening? Does it introduce the characters, the setting, or events well?
- ✓ Is your story well-organized? Do the events flow well?
- ✓ Does your story have an effective ending? Does it tie up the story well?
- ✓ Does your story include dialogue? If not, could dialogue make your story better?
- ✓ Have you used strong words? Are there words that could be replaced with better ones?
- ✓ Have you used effective descriptions? Could your descriptions be improved?
- ✓ Have you used sensory details? Could you add more sensory details to help readers imagine the scene?

Editing Checklist

- ✓ Have you used a variety of sentence structures? Are your sentences all written correctly?
- ✓ Is the grammar correct?
- ✓ Are all words spelled correctly? You can check the spelling of any words you are not sure of.
- ✓ Is punctuation used correctly?
- ✓ If dialogue is used, is it punctuated correctly?
- ✓ Are all words capitalized correctly?

Reading and Writing

Practice Set 5

This practice set contains four writing tasks. These are described below.

Task 1: Short Passage with Questions

This task has a short passage followed by questions. Read each question carefully. Then write your answer in the space provided.

You can also practice writing skills by completing the Core Writing Skills Practice exercise.

Task 2: Short Passage with Questions

This task has a short passage followed by questions. Read each question carefully. Then write your answer in the space provided.

You can also practice writing skills by completing the Core Writing Skills Practice exercise.

Task 3: Long Passage with Essay Question

This task has a longer passage with an essay question. Read the passage, complete the planning page, and then write or type your answer.

Task 4: Explanatory Writing Task

This final task requires you to write an essay that explains something. Read the writing prompt, complete the planning page, and then write or type your answer.

Task 1: Short Passage with Questions

The Stanley Cup

The Stanley Cup is the most appreciated ice hockey trophy in the world. It is awarded every year to the winner of the National Hockey League (NHL) championships.

Unlike most other sports, a new Stanley Cup is not made each year. Instead, the winning team keeps the trophy until new champions are crowned the next year. This ability to take possession of the trophy makes players appreciate the award even more. Each winning team also has the names of players, coaches, and other team staff engraved on the trophy. This is considered a great honor by all.

The Stanley Cup is the oldest professional sports trophy in North America. It was donated by the Governor General of Canada, Lord Stanley of Preston, in 1892.

CORE WRITING SKILLS PRACTICE
WRITE A RESEARCH REPORT

This passage gives information about the Stanley Cup. Another well-known trophy is called the Vince Lombardi Trophy. Research and write a short report about the Vince Lombardi Trophy. Include answers to the questions below in your report.

Who is the Vince Lombardi Trophy awarded to?

Who was Vince Lombardi?

What is the history of the Vince Lombardi Trophy?

1 Describe **three** facts given about the Stanley Cup.

Hint A fact is something that can be proven to be true.

1: _____

2: _____

3: _____

2 Describe **three** opinions given about the Stanley Cup.

Hint An opinion is something that cannot be proven. It is what someone thinks.

1: _____

2: _____

3: _____

Task 2: Short Passage with Questions

Snowed In

"HQ, this is Nord, do you copy?" Dr. Nord spoke into the microphone. He tapped away at various buttons and waited a few moments.

"Guess I'm stuck here for another day," Nord said as he hung his head.

Two days ago, a snow storm had hit the research bunker he was working in. The howling winds had battered against the walls of the bunker for hours, while snow had piled up and threatened to cover the bunker completely. Dr. Nord had stayed safely inside the research bunker. No matter how deafening the wind became or how hard the snow seemed to slam into the bunker, Dr. Nord remained calm. He knew that the bunker could withstand anything that the harsh weather could throw at it.

While the bunker stayed perfectly fine, the communications tower had been lost. Dr. Nord wasn't worried though. He knew someone would come looking for him.

CORE WRITING SKILLS PRACTICE

This passage is written from third person point of view. Imagine that the passage was written from first person point of view. Write a paragraph from Dr. Nord's point of view describing the storm.

_____

_____

_____

_____

_____

1. What do you think is the setting of the passage?

Hint: The passage does not tell you the setting, but it does give clues about the setting. Use the details from the passage to guess where Dr. Nord is, what season it is, and whether the events take place in the past, present, or future.

_____

_____

_____

_____

2. How does the author emphasize the severity of the storm? Use details from the passage in your answer.

_____

_____

_____

_____

3 What do you think will happen next in the passage? Use details from the passage to support your answer.

Hint: This question is asking you to make a prediction. Use the information given to guess what Dr. Nord will do next, or what will happen next. Be sure to use details from the passage to explain why you made that prediction.

Writing and Editing Checklist

After you finish writing your answer to question 3, you can use this guide to review and edit your work. Use the questions as a guide to finding ways you can improve your work.

Writing Checklist

- ✓ Have you described a prediction about what happens next?
- ✓ Does your prediction seem logical and make sense?
- ✓ Have you explained why you made that prediction and included details from the passage to support your prediction?
- ✓ Do your ideas flow well? Have you used words and phrases to link ideas well?

Editing Checklist

- ✓ Have you used a variety of sentence structures? Are your sentences all written correctly?
- ✓ Is the grammar correct?
- ✓ Are all words spelled correctly? You can check the spelling of any words you are not sure of.
- ✓ Is punctuation used correctly?
- ✓ If dialogue is used, is it punctuated correctly?
- ✓ Are all words capitalized correctly?

Task 3: Long Passage with Essay Question

Directions: Read the passage below. Then answer the question that follows. Use the planning page to plan your writing. Then write or type your essay.

A Man's Best Friend
by Damon Navarro

My dog is always smiling,
Come rain, hail, or shine.
His tail is always wagging,
Whether night or morning time.

He wakes me in the morning,
With the brush of his wet nose,
And lies beneath the covers,
Curled up tight beside my toes.

We go on winding morning walks,
Across the sunlit grounds,
He sniffs the scent of every plant,
And takes in every sound.

He enjoys everything around him,
With an endless sense of wonder,
And is not scared of anything,
Not rain, not noise, not thunder.

Throughout the day we mingle,
With other pups and folk,
He greets everyone with kindness,
You will never see him mope.

Or hide away from sunlight,
And long for evening rest,
He never, ever seeks his bed,
As man's best friend, he is the best.

Whether running through the fields,
Or playing with his toys,
He is a ray of constant sunshine,
And a perpetual source of joy.

When the nighttime tumbles,
And the darkness steals the light,
He offers gentle comfort,
Through the hours of every night.

In his sleep he dreams of daytime,
And spending time with me and others,
I am proud to call him my best friend,
My floppy-eared brother!

1.   What qualities of his dog do you think the author appreciates most? Use details from the poem to support your answer.

   In your answer, be sure to
   - identify the qualities of the dog that the author appreciates most
   - use details from the poem to support your answer
   - write an answer of between 1 and 2 pages

Hint

This question is asking you to draw a conclusion about how the author feels about his dog.

Read the poem again and focus on the positive qualities the author highlights. For example, in the first line the author says that the dog is "always smiling." This suggests that the author appreciates how happy and friendly the dog is.

Look for two or three positive qualities of the dog. Then plan your essay by focusing on each positive quality in turn. For each positive quality, you should include details from the poem that show that the author appreciates the quality.

Planning Page

Summary

Write a brief summary of what you are going to write about.

Supporting Details

Write down the facts, details, or examples you are going to include in your answer.

Outline

Write a plan for what you are going to write. Include the main points you want to cover and the order you will cover them.

Task 4: Explanatory Writing Task

Directions: Read the writing prompt below. Use the planning page to plan your writing. Then write or type your answer.

The Storm

The lightning flashed.
The thunder crashed.
The rain poured down.
I loved the sound.

In the poem, the poet describes a storm and seems to be enjoying the storm. Do you enjoy storms or do you find them scary? Write a composition explaining whether or not you like storms. Describe what you like or dislike about storms.

Hint

This writing task introduces the topic by using a poem. You do not have to refer to the poem in your answer. The poem is just there to help you start thinking about the topic.

The goal of your writing is to write about how you feel about storms. You will not be scored on whether or not you enjoy storms. You will be scored on how well you explain what you do or do not like about storms.

Planning Page

Summary

Write a brief summary of what you are going to write about.

Outline

Write a plan for what you are going to write. Include the main points you want to cover and the order you will cover them.

Writing and Editing Checklist

After you finish writing your essay, you can use this guide to review and edit your work. Use the questions as a guide to finding ways you can improve your work.

Writing Checklist

- ✓ Does your work have a strong opening? Does it introduce the topic and the main ideas?
- ✓ Is your work well-organized? Is related information grouped together? Does each paragraph have one main idea?
- ✓ Have you included facts, details, and examples to support your ideas?
- ✓ Is your work focused? Are there any details that do not fit with your main ideas?
- ✓ Do your ideas flow well? Have you used words and phrases to link ideas well?
- ✓ Does your work have a strong ending?

Editing Checklist

- ✓ Have you used a variety of sentence structures? Are your sentences all written correctly?
- ✓ Is the grammar correct?
- ✓ Are all words spelled correctly? You can check the spelling of any words you are not sure of.
- ✓ Is punctuation used correctly?
- ✓ Are all words capitalized correctly?

Reading and Writing

Practice Set 6

This practice set contains four writing tasks. These are described below.

Task 1: Short Passage with Questions

This task has a short passage followed by questions. Read each question carefully. Then write your answer in the space provided.

You can also practice writing skills by completing the Core Writing Skills Practice exercise.

Task 2: Short Passage with Questions

This task has a short passage followed by questions. Read each question carefully. Then write your answer in the space provided.

You can also practice writing skills by completing the Core Writing Skills Practice exercise.

Task 3: Short Story Writing Task

This task requires you to write a short story. Read the writing prompt, complete the planning page, and then write or type your answer.

Task 4: Argument Writing Task

This final task requires you to write an argument. Read the writing prompt, complete the planning page, and then write or type your answer.

Task 1: Short Passage with Questions

Making Money from Junk

It is possible to make money from almost anything. You can even earn money by collecting and selling scrap items to people. This can include collecting valuable metals, flooring, and various pieces of old home and office furniture that people no longer want. To make money from this, you do not need any cash to start with. You will only need a car and an adult to help you transport items.

To begin with, you will need to collect junk from homes and businesses. You can visit homes in your neighborhood. Knock on people's doors and ask if they would like any unwanted junk removed. You might put up flyers offering to remove unwanted items for people. Once you have a suitable collection of junk and scrap metals, it is time to sell it to buyers. You can place ads to sell your goods or you can contact places like scrap metal dealers.

There are important things to remember if you wish to make money from selling junk. The first is that while you can charge to remove waste, you also have to pay to dump it. Secondly, it is crucial that you understand the value of each metal and item that you try to sell. This will make sure that you sell your items for a fair price. Any items that you do not sell will need to be disposed of correctly. This will cost you a small fee to dump your waste or leave at a recycling depot.

**CORE WRITING SKILLS PRACTICE
WRITE AN ADVERTISEMENT**

Imagine that you have started the business described. You want to create a flyer to get people to allow you to take away unwanted items. List three main points you need to make in your flyer. Then create a flyer.

1. _____

2. _____

3. _____

1. Describe **two** problems you might encounter if you started the business described in the passage.

   Hint You can use a problem mentioned in the passage in your answer. You can also use a problem that you think of yourself.

   1: _____

   _____

   _____

   2: _____

   _____

   _____

2. Do you think the business described in the passage would be a good one to start? Explain why or why not.

   _____

   _____

   _____

   _____

   _____

Task 2: Short Passage with Questions

Troy McClure

Troy McClure is a reoccurring character in the popular television animation *The Simpsons*. He was created by writer Mike Reiss. The character was originally based on B-movie actors Troy Donahue and Doug McClure. Troy McClure was voiced by Phil Hartman, who died in 1998. Hartman's death led to the character being retired. It would have been possible to find someone else to be the voice of the character, but the show's producers decided to retire the character instead.

Troy McClure made his final appearance in the tenth season episode titled "Bart the Mother" in late 1989. It was a sad loss for a character that was much-loved by fans. Even though he played a relatively minor role in the show's plot, he is remembered well by fans and remains one of the show's most popular characters.

CORE WRITING SKILLS PRACTICE

Use the Internet to research who was the voice of each character in *The Simpsons*. Complete the chart with the name of the voice actors.

Character	Voice Actor
Homer Simpson	
Marge Simpson	
Bart Simpson	
Ned Flanders	

1. Complete the chart below by listing **three** people mentioned in the passage. Then list how each person was relevant to Troy McClure.

Person	How the Person was Relevant to Troy McClure

2. Describe **two** opinions from the passage.

 An opinion is something that cannot be proven. It is what someone thinks.

1: _____

_____

2: _____

_____

Task 3: Short Story Writing Task

Directions: Read the writing prompt below. Use the planning page to plan your writing. Then write or type your answer.

Look at the picture below.

Write a story based on what is happening in the picture.

The story shows a fairground. Your story should be based on the picture given, but you can take any direction you like. Your character could be lost at the fair, afraid to go on a ride, or tired of taking a younger sister on boring rides.

Focus on coming up with a character, a problem that the character's story will be based on, and a series of events that will solve the problem. This will ensure you have a complete story.

Planning Page

The Story
Write a summary of your story.

The Beginning
Describe what is going to happen at the start of your story.

The Middle
Describe what is going to happen in the middle of your story.

The End
Describe what is going to happen at the end of your story.

Task 4: Argument Writing Task

Directions: Read the writing prompt below. Use the planning page to plan your writing. Then write or type your answer.

Read this proverb about actions.

> Don't try to walk before you can crawl.

Think about what this proverb tells you about taking things slowly. Write an article for your school newspaper in which you give students this advice. Use facts, details, or examples in your answer.

Hint

A proverb is a short saying that states an idea. The idea in this proverb is that you should not try difficult things until you are ready. You should use this as the main argument in your article.

To make this argument, you will need ideas to support it. You can base this on your personal experience. For example, try to think of a time where you tried something before you were ready. If you can't think of how this happened to you, you could also think about how it happened to someone you know. Focus on describing 2 or 3 examples of how this proverb relates to events that have happened to you or to people you know.

Planning Page

Summary

Write a brief summary of your claim.

Supporting Details

Write down the facts, details, or examples you are going to include.

Outline

Write a plan for what you are going to write. Include the main points you want to cover and the order you will cover them.

Writing and Editing Checklist

After you finish writing your argument, you can use this guide to review and edit your work. Use the questions as a guide to finding ways you can improve your work.

Writing Checklist

- ✓ Does your work have one clear claim?
- ✓ Does your work have a strong opening? Does the opening introduce the topic and state the claim?
- ✓ Is your claim supported? Have you used clear reasons to support your claim?
- ✓ Have you used enough evidence? Is your evidence all relevant?
- ✓ Is your work well-organized? Is related information grouped together? Does each paragraph have one main idea?
- ✓ Do your ideas flow well? Have you used words and phrases to link ideas well?
- ✓ Does your work have a strong ending? Does the ending restate the main idea and tie up the argument?

Editing Checklist

- ✓ Have you used a variety of sentence structures? Are your sentences all written correctly?
- ✓ Is the grammar correct?
- ✓ Are all words spelled correctly? You can check the spelling of any words you are not sure of.
- ✓ Is punctuation used correctly?
- ✓ Are all words capitalized correctly?

Writing Skills Workbook, IAR Guided Practice, Grade 7

Reading and Writing

Practice Set 7

This practice set contains four writing tasks. These are described below.

Task 1: Short Passage with Questions

This task has a short passage followed by questions. Read each question carefully. Then write your answer in the space provided.

Task 2: Short Passage with Questions

This task has a short passage followed by questions. Read each question carefully. Then write your answer in the space provided.

You can also practice writing skills by completing the Core Writing Skills Practice exercise.

Task 3: Long Passage with Essay Question

This task has a longer passage with an essay question. Read the passage, complete the planning page, and then write or type your answer.

Task 4: Explanatory Writing Task

This final task requires you to write an essay that explains something. Read the writing prompt, complete the planning page, and then write or type your answer.

Task 1: Short Passage with Questions

The Human Skeleton

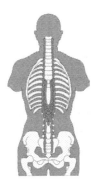

Did you know that there are over 206 bones in the adult human skeleton? Newborn babies have over 270 bones. As a newborn baby grows, some of their bones are fused together.

The skeleton performs several very important functions. These include providing a support framework, protecting vital organs, and playing a crucial role in the generation of blood cells. Bones are also a storage site for many of the minerals our bodies need.

Osteoporosis is a medical condition that occurs when the bones become less dense. This makes them weak and brittle, and can lead to bones fracturing easily. When a bone is very brittle, something as simple as coughing can result in a fracture. Osteoporosis can affect anyone, but is most common in women. Luckily, preventing osteoporosis is quite simple.

Three Simple Rules

1. Have a Diet High in Calcium
Your body needs calcium to keep your bones strong. Calcium is found in dairy products, leafy green vegetables, and soy products.

2. Get Enough Vitamin D
Your body uses sunlight to make vitamin D. As long as you spend a normal amount of time outdoors, your body should be getting enough vitamin D. Vitamin D is also found in salmon, tuna, sardines, and eggs.

3. Exercise
Regular exercise will keep your bones strong and healthy. Walking, running, jogging, and skipping are all good for the health of your bones.

1. How does the information in the second paragraph help show the importance of looking after your bones? Explain your answer.

___

2. Why does the author include the section titled "Three Simple Rules"?

Hint: To answer this question, explain the purpose of this section and how it relates to the rest of the passage.

___

Task 2: Short Passage with Questions

Drummer Boy

Tap-tap-tap, ratta-tat-tat. Tim used his two pencils on his school desk like drumsticks. He hummed his favorite tune as he enjoyed daydreaming. A few students glared at him, but Tim didn't even notice. He just kept playing his song, while imagining he was on stage in front of hoards of screaming fans. Tim's drumming became louder and louder as he continued playing for the imaginary crowd. The classroom became silent as everyone stared at Tim. In his mind, the silence was the crowd waiting for his final drum solo. Mr. Paulson turned around from writing on the board.

"Tim! Would you cut that out?" Mr. Paulson hollered.

Tim nearly jumped out of his chair as he came back to reality. He looked around the room, and realized that all eyes were on him. Unlike in his daydream, they were not marveling at his musical talent.

"Sorry about that, sir!" Tim said as all the other kids chuckled a little.

Mr. Paulson went back to writing on the board. Tim opened his notebook and wrote in it. *One day I'm going to be in a band*, he wrote.

CORE WRITING SKILLS PRACTICE

How does the first paragraph show that Tim is focused on his daydream?

_____

_____

_____

_____

1   Why does the author say that Tim "nearly jumped out of his chair"?

_____

_____

_____

_____

_____

2   How do you think the students in the class felt about Tim's drumming?

Hint: You can use information in the passage to answer this question. You can also use your personal opinion. For example, you could write about how you think you would feel if someone in your class was drumming like Tim was.

_____

_____

_____

_____

_____

Writing Skills Workbook, IAR Guided Practice, Grade 7

Task 3: Long Passage with Essay Question

Directions: Read the passage below. Then answer the question that follows. Use the planning page to plan your writing. Then write or type your essay.

Truth and Lies

Connor's parents were very fair minded. They did not believe in harsh or unnecessary rules. One rule they did have was that Connor and his brother Michael were not allowed to play ball indoors. Nevertheless, it was not unknown for them to play the occasional game when their parents were outside or working in the garden. One day Connor suggested playing while his father was mowing the lawn and his mother was out shopping.

"I don't know Connor," said Michael. "Dad's just outside."

"It won't hurt," said Connor persuasively. "We will only play a quick game."

As Connor was his older brother by two years, Michael agreed. He went and got a ball and they began to pass the ball between them. Once they played for a moment or two, they began to get far more competitive. They assigned goals and began to compete for points.

"Right then," said Connor as he took control of the ball. "The first one to score five goals wins."

Michael nodded in agreement. Connor dropped the ball and struck it fiercely towards his brother. Michael raised his arm to hit the ball back.

The ball spun to the left and hit a vase on the side table. Both Connor and Michael paused as the vase tumbled to the ground. It shattered on the dining room floor. The two brothers looked at each other in stunned silence.

"What now?" asked Michael.

Before Connor could respond, his father came running into the house through the back door. He had clearly heard the noise as the vase fell. As he stopped, he noticed the broken vase and the ball sitting on the floor nearby.

"What have your mother and I told you both about playing ball inside?" he asked angrily. "Who was it? Who broke the vase?"

There was a pause as Connor and Michael exchanged glances. Michael clearly didn't want to blame his brother even though he touched the ball last before it hit the vase. Connor considered saying his brother was responsible. He was about to say his brother's name when he noticed how alarmed Michael's expression was. Then he remembered that his mother had always said that it was better to tell the truth than to lie. He sighed as he began to speak.

"It was me, Dad. It was my idea to play and it is my fault that the vase broke."

"Thank you Connor," he said as he began to collect the broken pieces of the vase. "I know you were in the wrong, but I appreciate you being honest."

Connor then bent down and began to help his father clean up the mess.

"I am sorry, Dad," he said softly. "It won't happen again."

1. The passage describes a boy who is tempted to lie, but then tells the truth. Think of a time when you were tempted to lie. Explain whether or not you lied, and what happened because you lied or because you told the truth.

   In your answer, be sure to
   - describe a time when you were tempted to lie
   - explain whether or not you lied
   - describe what happened because you lied or because you told the truth
   - write an answer of between 1 and 2 pages

The question asks you to relate to the passage. You have to write about your own experience in being tempted to lie. Start by thinking of one particular situation when you were tempted to lie. It could be a time you thought about lying, but then told the truth. It could also be a time when you did lie. Write about that time and what happened.

This question is asking about your own personal experience, so you can also include your thoughts on the decision you made.

Planning Page

Summary

Write a brief summary of what you are going to write about.

Outline

Write a plan for what you are going to write. Include the main points you want to cover and the order you will cover them.

Task 4: Explanatory Writing Task

Directions: Read the writing prompt below. Use the planning page to plan your writing. Then write or type your answer.

Everyone has strengths and weaknesses. What is your greatest strength and your greatest weakness?

Write an essay describing your greatest strength and your greatest weakness. Explain why each quality is a strength or a weakness.

Hint

This question is asking about your personal qualities. A strength could be determination, your positive attitude, or how you work well as part of a team. A weakness could be that you like everything to be perfect, that you worry too much, or that you are sometimes lazy.

The key to gaining full marks on this question is to identify a weakness and a strength and to describe each well. You should not only describe the quality, but should also explain how it affects you. For the strength, explain how it benefits you. For the weakness, explain how it limits you. Use specific examples to clearly explain why each quality is a strength or a weakness.

Planning Page

Summary

Write a brief summary of what you are going to write about.

Outline

Write a plan for what you are going to write. Include the main points you want to cover and the order you will cover them.

Writing and Editing Checklist

After you finish writing your essay, you can use this guide to review and edit your work. Use the questions as a guide to finding ways you can improve your work.

Writing Checklist

- ✓ Does your work have a strong opening? Does it introduce the topic and the main ideas?
- ✓ Is your work well-organized? Is related information grouped together? Does each paragraph have one main idea?
- ✓ Have you included facts, details, and examples to support your ideas?
- ✓ Is your work focused? Are there any details that do not fit with your main ideas?
- ✓ Do your ideas flow well? Have you used words and phrases to link ideas well?
- ✓ Does your work have a strong ending?

Editing Checklist

- ✓ Have you used a variety of sentence structures? Are your sentences all written correctly?
- ✓ Is the grammar correct?
- ✓ Are all words spelled correctly? You can check the spelling of any words you are not sure of.
- ✓ Is punctuation used correctly?
- ✓ Are all words capitalized correctly?

Reading and Writing

Practice Set 8

This practice set contains four writing tasks. These are described below.

Task 1: Short Passage with Questions

This task has a short passage followed by questions. Read each question carefully. Then write your answer in the space provided.

You can also practice writing skills by completing the Core Writing Skills Practice exercise.

Task 2: Short Passage with Questions

This task has a short passage followed by questions. Read each question carefully. Then write your answer in the space provided.

You can also practice writing skills by completing the Core Writing Skills Practice exercise.

Task 3: Argument Writing Task

This task requires you to write an argument. Read the writing prompt, complete the planning page, and then write or type your answer.

Task 4: Short Story Writing Task

This task requires you to write a short story. Read the writing prompt, complete the planning page, and then write or type your answer.

Task 1: Short Passage with Questions

Magnetic North

The compass was invented in ancient China around 247 B.C. It became popular for use in navigation by the 11th century. In those early days, they were an essential tool for sailors and explorers. Militaries also relied on them for land navigation, or orienteering. Today, compasses are still used by some sailors, but are not as important as they once were. New technologies have replaced the compass in many ways. Sailors now often use computerized systems and GPS to navigate. Computerized compasses will tell you the direction faster and more accurately than an actual compass. Many cell phones even have built-in compasses. Even with these technologies, learning to use a compass is a very useful skill. They are often used by people doing activities like hiking or orienteering.

Most compass devices consist of a dial with north, east, south, and west marked on them. The compass has a spinning needle mounted in the middle. The needle is magnetized and aligns itself with the Earth's magnetic field. This results in the compass needle always facing toward the north.

CORE SKILLS PRACTICE

What benefits do computerized compasses have over regular compasses? What disadvantages do you think computerized compasses might have?

_____

_____

_____

_____

_____

1. The author states that even with new technologies, "learning to use a compass is a very useful skill." Does the author include enough information to support this claim? Explain your answer.

_____

_____

_____

_____

_____

_____

2. Why are compasses less important to sailors today than they once were?

Hint — Use information from the passage to explain why compasses are not as necessary today as they once were.

_____

_____

_____

_____

_____

_____

Task 2: Short Passage with Questions

The Astronomer

An astronomer used to go out at night to observe the stars. One evening, he was wandering around town with his eyes fixed on the sky. He suddenly tripped and fell into a well. He sat there and groaned about his sores and bruises and cried for help. He pummeled his fists against the well. He looked up and all he could see were the stars. The twinkling stars looked back down on him and laughed.

The astronomer's friend finally heard his cries and made his way over to the well. After hearing the astronomer's story of how he fell, he simply shook his head.

"Old friend, in striving to see into the heavens, you don't manage to see what is on the earth," the friend said.

CORE WRITING SKILLS PRACTICE
WRITE A SHORT STORY

This passage is based on a fable written by Aesop. The main purpose of a fable is to teach readers a lesson. Choose one of the lessons or morals listed below. Write your own fable that will teach people this lesson.

Honesty is the best policy.

Appearances can be deceiving.

Slow and steady wins the race.

There is always someone worse off than yourself.

There are two sides to every story.

Pride comes before a fall.

1. What lesson does the astronomer learn in the passage? Explain your answer.

2. Identify the personification used in the passage and explain why the author included it.

Hint Personification is a literary technique where objects are given human qualities, or described as if they are human.

3 Think about the lesson the astronomer learns in the passage. How could this lesson apply to your own life?

Hint — Start by identifying the lesson the astronomer learns. This is related to the theme of the passage. Then describe how you could use this lesson in your own life.

_____

_____

_____

_____

_____

_____

_____

_____

_____

_____

_____

_____

Writing and Editing Checklist

After you finish writing your answer to question 3, you can use this guide to review and edit your work. Use the questions as a guide to finding ways you can improve your work.

Writing Checklist

- ✓ Does your work have a strong opening? Does it introduce the topic and the main ideas?
- ✓ Is your work well-organized? Is related information grouped together? Does each paragraph have one main idea?
- ✓ Have you clearly explained what the astronomer learns?
- ✓ Have you clearly explained how you could use the lesson in your own life?
- ✓ Is your work focused? Are there any details that do not fit with your main ideas?
- ✓ Do your ideas flow well? Have you used words and phrases to link ideas well?

Editing Checklist

- ✓ Have you used a variety of sentence structures? Are your sentences all written correctly?
- ✓ Is the grammar correct?
- ✓ Are all words spelled correctly? You can check the spelling of any words you are not sure of.
- ✓ Is punctuation used correctly?
- ✓ If dialogue is used, is it punctuated correctly?
- ✓ Are all words capitalized correctly?

Task 3: Argument Writing Task

Directions: Read the writing prompt below. Use the planning page to plan your writing. Then write or type your answer.

Your town wants to encourage people to use public transport. They are considering charging a fee to park a car on all streets in the city area. They think this will encourage people to use buses and trains more.

Write a letter to your local newspaper giving your opinion on whether or not the parking fee is a good idea. Use reasons, facts, and/or examples to support your position.

Hint

A letter written to persuade needs to use good supporting details. You should state your opinion of whether the parking fee is a good idea or a bad idea. You should then give reasons to support your opinion.

If you are against the parking fee, you should focus on the problems it will cause. If you are for the parking fee, you should describe the benefits.

The key to a good persuasive letter is to use specific examples and details that will help readers understand your opinion and agree with it.

Planning Page

Summary

Write a brief summary of your claim.

Supporting Details

Write down the facts, details, or examples you are going to include.

Outline

Write a plan for what you are going to write. Include the main points you want to cover and the order you will cover them.

Task 4: Short Story Writing Task

Directions: Read the writing prompt below. Use the planning page to plan your writing. Then write or type your answer.

Look at the picture below.

Write a story based on what is happening in the picture.

A good short story will often have a main theme or a message to communicate. The events in the story will be designed to communicate this message.

This writing prompt could be used to write a serious story about a skater's struggle to win. The theme of this story could be about whether sacrifices are worth it. The prompt could also be used to write an inspiring story about hard work paying off. Another idea is that the winning skater is cheating in some way. The theme of this story could be about honesty or sportsmanship.

As you plan your story, think of a message that you want to focus on. You do not have to state the message in your story, but the events should make readers think about the message.

Planning Page

The Story
Write a summary of your story.

The Beginning
Describe what is going to happen at the start of your story.

The Middle
Describe what is going to happen in the middle of your story.

The End
Describe what is going to happen at the end of your story.

Writing and Editing Checklist

After you finish writing your story, you can use this guide to review and edit your work. Use the questions as a guide to finding ways you can improve your work.

Writing Checklist

- ✓ Does your story have a strong opening? Does it introduce the characters, the setting, or events well?
- ✓ Is your story well-organized? Do the events flow well?
- ✓ Does your story have an effective ending? Does it tie up the story well?
- ✓ Does your story include dialogue? If not, could dialogue make your story better?
- ✓ Have you used strong words? Are there words that could be replaced with better ones?
- ✓ Have you used effective descriptions? Could your descriptions be improved?
- ✓ Have you used sensory details? Could you add more sensory details to help readers imagine the scene?

Editing Checklist

- ✓ Have you used a variety of sentence structures? Are your sentences all written correctly?
- ✓ Is the grammar correct?
- ✓ Are all words spelled correctly? You can check the spelling of any words you are not sure of.
- ✓ Is punctuation used correctly?
- ✓ If dialogue is used, is it punctuated correctly?
- ✓ Are all words capitalized correctly?

Reading and Writing

Practice Set 9

This practice set contains four writing tasks. These are described below.

Task 1: Short Passage with Questions

This task has a short passage followed by questions. Read each question carefully. Then write your answer in the space provided.

You can also practice writing skills by completing the Core Writing Skills Practice exercise.

Task 2: Short Passage with Questions

This task has a short passage followed by questions. Read each question carefully. Then write your answer in the space provided.

You can also practice writing skills by completing the Core Writing Skills Practice exercise.

Task 3: Long Passage with Essay Question

This task has a longer passage with an essay question. Read the passage, complete the planning page, and then write or type your answer.

Task 4: Personal Narrative Writing Task

This final task requires you to write a personal narrative. Read the writing prompt, complete the planning page, and then write or type your answer.

Task 1: Short Passage with Questions

Ruler of Macedon

Alexander the Great is one of the most noteworthy kings of all time. He was king of Macedon in north-eastern Greece in 336 B.C. By the age of 30, Alexander the Great had created one of the largest empires in ancient history. He was responsible for the fall of the Persian king Darius III, among many other grand accomplishments. The tactical achievements of Alexander are still taught throughout the world in military academies today.

This 1895 painting shows Alexander the Great being tutored by Aristotle.

**CORE WRITING SKILLS PRACTICE
WRITE A RESEARCH REPORT**

This passage is a short biography of Alexander the Great. Choose another famous leader from the list below. Research and write a short biography of that person.

Charlemagne
Attila the Hun
Constantine
King Henry VIII
Genghis Khan

1. Explain how you can tell that the author admires Alexander the Great.

   Hint: Focus on the achievements described and the words the author uses to describe Alexander the Great.

   _____
   _____
   _____
   _____
   _____

2. Identify **two** significant achievements of Alexander the Great.

   1: _____
   _____

   2: _____
   _____

Task 2: Short Passage with Questions

The Dwarf Miner

The dwarf picked up a lump of gold from the ground. He stared at it for a few moments and then bit it sharply between his teeth.

"She sure is gold!" he proclaimed excitedly, before picking up his pickaxe.

The dwarf wandered around in front of the rock wall for a few minutes, before swinging his tool into it. After a few hours of mining, the dwarf had a small bowl full of gleaming golden nuggets. He set off happily for home, whistling all the way there.

CORE WRITING SKILLS PRACTICE

Imagine that someone tries to rob the dwarf of his gold as he is going home. Continue the story by writing a paragraph describing the robbery.

_____

_____

_____

_____

_____

_____

_____

1. Why do you think the dwarf bites the lump of gold he picks up?

   Hint — Use the information in the passage to make an inference about why the dwarf does this.

   _____
   _____
   _____
   _____

2. Write a summary of the events of the passage.

   Hint — A summary should describe the main events of a passage. It should include only the important events or details.

   _____
   _____
   _____
   _____
   _____

Task 3: Long Passage with Essay Question

Directions: Read the passage below. Then answer the question that follows. Use the planning page to plan your writing. Then write or type your essay.

Taking the Lead

Thomas was a very competitive person. He always did his utmost to win every game, race, or challenge. His favorite sport was athletics. Ever since he had been a child, he had enjoyed sprinting. He had won a number of events at the last regional sports day. Thomas represented his school regularly. He also trained very hard for each and every event. He took his preparation very seriously. He dreamed that one day he would be a professional athlete competing in the Olympic Games.

His attitude, however, didn't win him many friends. He sometimes insulted fellow competitors by laughing when they lost or calling them names. On the rare occasions Thomas lost, he did not shake his rival's hand or congratulate anyone who had finished ahead of him. Both his parents and his teachers told him that part of winning was learning how to also lose with grace. Despite this, he chose to ignore their advice and continue along the same paths as before. Many of Thomas' rivals despised his behavior. They wished he would be more considerate towards his fellow competitors.

One day, Thomas was in a race against a rival school. They were competing for the top regional trophy. In the first event, Thomas had won but suffered a small strain to his right knee. His coach and the team doctor examined the injury and suggested that he sit out of the final race. Thomas refused to listen to their suggestions.

"You should sit this out," explained his doctor carefully. "If you race, you may not only lose but you could make the injury far worse."

Thomas shook his head defiantly.

"I am fine. If I don't race our school has *no* chance of winning."

Thomas' teammates were insulted by his statement. However, Thomas was allowed to compete. When the race started, Thomas decided to set off at a very quick pace. This was unusual as he liked to pace himself and accelerate at the close of the race. His injury inspired him to start quickly and get a solid lead. After the first lap, he was far in front of everyone else. His lead actually increased over the next lap, too. Then it happened. He felt a sharp and sudden pain in his knee before he felt himself starting to fall. He tried to regain his balance but his injured knee couldn't hold him any longer.

Thomas officially came last in the race and had to be carried off the track. He was very quiet as he lay still in the changing rooms.

"You've strained your knee quite badly," said the doctor. "You will need to rest it for a few weeks."

Thomas looked at his teammates looking on.

"I am sorry," he said to his teammates as they gathered around him. "I let you all down."

He expected his teammates to be mad at him, but they only seemed concerned about his health. Thomas imagined what he might have done if someone else in the team had tried to run with an injury. He imagined that he would be furious. He suddenly realized how selfish he had been. From that day forward, Thomas vowed to be a better sportsman and use his competitive nature to benefit his team.

1. What do you think is the main message of the passage? How could you use this message in your own life? Use details from the passage in your answer.

   In your answer, be sure to
   - describe the main message of the passage
   - relate the main message to your own life
   - use details from the passage in your answer
   - write an answer of between 1 and 2 pages

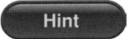

There are two parts to this writing task. You should start by describing what the message of the passage is. This is the lesson that Thomas learns, and also the lesson that readers learn.

After describing the message, you should write about how it relates to you. Write a paragraph or two describing how you could use the message to help you in your own life. It could be related to sport, or to any other relevant part of your life.

Planning Page

Summary

Write a brief summary of what you are going to write about.

Supporting Details

Write down the facts, details, or examples you are going to include in your answer.

Outline

Write a plan for what you are going to write. Include the main points you want to cover and the order you will cover them.

Task 4: Personal Narrative Writing Task

Directions: Read the writing prompt below. Use the planning page to plan your writing. Then write or type your answer.

Read this quote about defeat.

> What is defeat? Nothing but education; nothing but the first step to something better.
> -Wendell Phillips

Write a composition describing a time when you were defeated. Explain what you learned from your defeat.

Hint

The quote in this writing prompt introduces the idea that defeat can be used as a learning experience. In your writing, you should write about how this idea relates to you. Your answer should be based on your personal experience.

Think of a situation where you were defeated, but learned from the experience. Be sure to give details about the defeat so the reader will understand your experience. Then be sure to also describe what you learned or how you changed.

Planning Page

Summary

Write a brief summary of what you are going to write about.

Outline

Write a plan for what you are going to write. Include the main points you want to cover and the order you will cover them.

Writing and Editing Checklist

After you finish writing your personal narrative, you can use this guide to review and edit your work. Use the questions as a guide to finding ways you can improve your work.

Writing Checklist

- ✓ Does your work have a strong opening? Does it introduce the main ideas or set the scene well?
- ✓ Is your work well-organized? Is related information grouped together? Does each paragraph have one main idea?
- ✓ Does your work have an effective ending? Does it tie up the events well?
- ✓ Is your work focused? Are there any details that do not fit with your main ideas?
- ✓ Do your ideas flow well? Have you used words and phrases to link ideas well?
- ✓ Have you used strong words? Are there words that could be replaced with better ones?
- ✓ Have you used effective descriptions? Could your descriptions be improved?
- ✓ Have you used sensory details? Could you add more sensory details to help readers imagine the scene?

Editing Checklist

- ✓ Have you used a variety of sentence structures? Are your sentences all written correctly?
- ✓ Is the grammar correct?
- ✓ Are all words spelled correctly? You can check the spelling of any words you are not sure of.
- ✓ Is punctuation used correctly?
- ✓ If dialogue is used, is it punctuated correctly?
- ✓ Are all words capitalized correctly?

Reading and Writing

Practice Set 10

This practice set contains four writing tasks. These are described below.

Task 1: Short Passage with Questions

This task has a short passage followed by questions. Read each question carefully. Then write your answer in the space provided.

You can also practice writing skills by completing the Core Writing Skills Practice exercise.

Task 2: Short Passage with Questions

This task has a short passage followed by questions. Read each question carefully. Then write your answer in the space provided.

You can also practice writing skills by completing the Core Writing Skills Practice exercise.

Task 3: Short Story Writing Task

This task requires you to write a short story. Read the writing prompt, complete the planning page, and then write or type your answer.

Task 4: Argument Writing Task

This final task requires you to write an argument. Read the writing prompt, complete the planning page, and then write or type your answer.

Writing Skills Workbook, IAR Guided Practice, Grade 7

Task 1: Short Passage with Questions

The Park

Dear Diary,

Today Mom and I went for a walk in the park after school. The park is such a pretty and peaceful place with all of those trees, flowers, and birds. We saw people having picnics, and some kids rowing boats on the lake. Some people were also feeding bread to the ducks.

We saw one man who was painted in silver paint. He was standing completely still and changing his pose every few minutes. While he was still, he looked exactly like a statue! It was pretty amazing to watch. Mom and I took a photo in front of him. We said goodbye and left some change in his tip jar. What a great afternoon!

Harmanie

CORE WRITING SKILLS PRACTICE

The park is one of Harmanie's favorite places. Think of a place that you enjoy spending time. Write a paragraph explaining why you like spending time there.

_____

_____

_____

_____

_____

1 Circle the word that you think best describes Harmanie's afternoon. Then explain why you made that choice.

        exciting   **relaxing**   **tedious**

_____

_____

_____

_____

2 Describe **three** things that Harmanie saw people doing in the park.

Things that Harmanie Saw People Doing in the Park
1)
2)
3)

Task 2: Short Passage with Questions

The Desert Oasis

Serian had walked for days in the desert. He wasn't sure if he would ever see anyone again. Serian was lost. He scuffled across the hot desert sand, waiting for nightfall to ease the sweltering heat. Serian reached the peak of a sand dune. He planted himself on the hot sand and took a few moments to rest his weary body.

As he stared off into the distance, he noticed something glimmering. He shielded his eyes from the harsh desert light and tried to focus his eyes. He saw an oasis filled with plants and a large lake. Serian closed his eyes and shook his head back and forth, as if testing to see if the image would shake loose. When he opened his eyes, the oasis was still there. He smiled for the first time in days as he powered on toward the oasis.

CORE SKILLS PRACTICE

Sensory details can help readers imagine a scene. Write a description of the desert that helps readers imagine how hot it is. You might describe the feeling of the hot sand on your feet or the feeling of sweat on your forehead. Use sensory details to help readers imagine the heat.

_____

_____

_____

_____

_____

1. How does the author create a mood of hopelessness in the first paragraph?

   Hint — The mood of a passage is the way the passage makes the reader feel. It is the atmosphere of the passage.

   _____
   _____
   _____
   _____

2. What do you think will happen next in the passage?

   Hint — This question is asking you to make a prediction. At the end of the passage, Serian is walking toward the oasis. Write about what you think will happen when he reaches it.

   _____
   _____
   _____
   _____

3 How do Serian's feelings change in the passage? What is the turning point that causes his feelings to change?

Hint Start by describing Serian's feelings at the start of the passage. Then describe the turning point of the passage. Finish by describing his feelings at the end of the passage.

Writing and Editing Checklist

After you finish writing your answer to question 3, you can use this guide to review and edit your work. Use the questions as a guide to finding ways you can improve your work.

Writing Checklist

- ✓ Does your work have a strong opening? Does it introduce the topic and the main ideas?
- ✓ Is your work well-organized? Is related information grouped together? Does each paragraph have one main idea?
- ✓ Have you clearly explained Serian's feelings? Have you used details from the passage to support your claims?
- ✓ Is your work focused? Are there any details that do not fit with your main ideas?
- ✓ Do your ideas flow well? Have you used words and phrases to link ideas well?

Editing Checklist

- ✓ Have you used a variety of sentence structures? Are your sentences all written correctly?
- ✓ Is the grammar correct?
- ✓ Are all words spelled correctly? You can check the spelling of any words you are not sure of.
- ✓ Is punctuation used correctly?
- ✓ If dialogue is used, is it punctuated correctly?
- ✓ Are all words capitalized correctly?

Task 3: Short Story Writing Task

Directions: Read the writing prompt below. Use the planning page to plan your writing. Then write or type your answer.

Corey walked through the museum's doors. He was surprised to find that there wasn't a single person there. He decided it was time to explore. He was about to have a very interesting adventure.

Write a story about Corey's adventure in the museum.

Hint

Remember that in a story you are writing, anything can happen! You do not have to write about things that could happen in real life. You can make up strange, exciting, and impossible events. As you plan this story, ask yourself what amazing thing could happen to Corey. Then focus your story on one amazing event that occurs.

Planning Page

The Story
Write a summary of your story.

The Beginning
Describe what is going to happen at the start of your story.

The Middle
Describe what is going to happen in the middle of your story.

The End
Describe what is going to happen at the end of your story.

Task 4: Argument Writing Task

Directions: Read the writing prompt below. Use the planning page to plan your writing. Then write or type your answer.

Your school is planning to introduce a new policy to encourage students to read. All students will have to read two novels each month. Students are expected to do the reading outside of school hours. There has been some debate about the policy. Some people think it is important and worthwhile, while others think that students should be free to choose whether they want to read in their spare time.

Write a letter to your school newspaper giving your opinion on whether or not the new policy is a good idea. Use reasons, facts, and/or examples to support your position.

Hint

When completing these writing tasks, it is important to include supporting details. In some tasks, you can use facts. In a task like this, it is often better to use details and examples.

You should think about how this policy will affect you. You could describe how it would benefit you, or why it would not be good for you. Be sure to use specific examples of how the policy will affect you.

Planning Page

Summary

Write a brief summary of your claim.

Supporting Details

Write down the facts, details, or examples you are going to include.

Outline

Write a plan for what you are going to write. Include the main points you want to cover and the order you will cover them.

Writing and Editing Checklist

After you finish writing your argument, you can use this guide to review and edit your work. Use the questions as a guide to finding ways you can improve your work.

Writing Checklist

- ✓ Does your work have one clear claim?
- ✓ Does your work have a strong opening? Does the opening introduce the topic and state the claim?
- ✓ Is your claim supported? Have you used clear reasons to support your claim?
- ✓ Have you used enough evidence? Is your evidence all relevant?
- ✓ Is your work well-organized? Is related information grouped together? Does each paragraph have one main idea?
- ✓ Do your ideas flow well? Have you used words and phrases to link ideas well?
- ✓ Does your work have a strong ending? Does the ending restate the main idea and tie up the argument?

Editing Checklist

- ✓ Have you used a variety of sentence structures? Are your sentences all written correctly?
- ✓ Is the grammar correct?
- ✓ Are all words spelled correctly? You can check the spelling of any words you are not sure of.
- ✓ Is punctuation used correctly?
- ✓ Are all words capitalized correctly?

Answer Key

Developing Reading and Writing Skills

The state of Illinois has adopted the Illinois Learning Standards. Student learning throughout the year is based on these standards, and all the questions on the state tests assess these standards. All the questions and exercises in this workbook are based on the knowledge and skills described in the Illinois Learning Standards. While this workbook focuses specifically on the writing standards, the questions based on passages also assess reading standards.

Core Skills Practice Exercises

Each short passage in this workbook includes an exercise focused on one key skill described in the Illinois Learning Standards. The answer key identifies the core skill covered by each exercise, and describes what to look for in the student's response.

Scoring Constructed-Response Questions

The short passages in this workbook include constructed-response questions, where students provide a written answer to a question. The answer key gives guidance on how to score these questions. Use the criteria listed as a guide to scoring these questions, and as a guide for giving the student advice on how to improve an answer.

Scoring Writing Tasks

The writing tasks in this workbook are scored based on rubrics that list the features expected of student writing. These features are based on the skills described in the Illinois Learning Standards. The rubrics used for scoring these questions are included in the back of this book. Use the rubric to score these questions, and as a guide for giving the student advice on how to improve an answer.

Writing Skills Workbook, IAR Guided Practice, Grade 7

Practice Set 1

Task 1: Short Passage with Questions (The Dog and the River)

Core Writing Skills Practice
Core skill: Draw evidence from literary texts to support analysis, reflection, and research.
Answer: The student should explain how the lesson from the passage could be applied to his or her own life. The lesson should be about appreciating what you have, not being jealous of what others have, or another valid lesson related to the events of the passage.

Q1. Give a score of 0, 1, or 2 based on how well the answer meets the criteria listed.
- It should identify the passage as being a fable.
- It should give relevant evidence. The evidence could include that the main character is a dog, that the dog learns a lesson, or that the passage has a moral.

Q2. Give a score of 0, 1, or 2 based on how well the answer meets the criteria listed.
- It should refer to how the dog seems upset, disappointed, or frustrated.
- It may refer to how the dog struck at his reflection with his paw or how he stared sadly as the meat floated away.

Task 2: Short Passage with Questions (Understanding Genius)

Core Writing Skills Practice
Core skill: Draw evidence from informational texts to support analysis, reflection, and research.
Answer: The student should describe the information gained from studying Einstein's brain.

Q1. Give a score of 0, 1, or 2 based on how well the answer meets the criteria listed.
- It should explain the relevance of the title to the content of the passage.
- It may refer to Einstein as a genius, and refer to how his brain was studied to try to understand his great intelligence.

Q2. Give a score of 0, 1, or 2 based on how well the answer meets the criteria listed.
- It should give an opinion on whether the actions of Dr. Thomas Harvey were reasonable.
- Either opinion is acceptable as long as it is well-supported.
- The student may argue that it was not right to study Einstein's brain without permission from the family, or that the benefits of studying Einstein's brain were worth it.

Task 3: Long Passage with Essay Question

Use the Informative/Explanatory Writing Rubric to review the work and give a score out of 4.

Task 4: Personal Narrative Writing Task

Use the Narrative Writing Rubric to review the work and give a score out of 4.

Practice Set 2

Task 1: Short Passage with Questions (Bananas)

Core Writing Skills Practice

Core skill: Write informative/explanatory texts to examine a topic and convey ideas, concepts, and information through the selection, organization, and analysis of relevant content.
Answer: The student should write a set of instructions describing how to open a banana. The instructions should be clear, easy to understand, and in sequence.

Q1. Give a score of 0, 1, or 2 based on how well the answer meets the criteria listed.
- It should explain that the phrase "messing with me" refers to someone joking or trying to trick someone into believing something.

Q2. Give a score of 0, 1, or 2 based on how well the answer meets the criteria listed.
- It should compare how Harmanie opens bananas to how monkeys open bananas.

Task 2: Short Passage with Questions (Antique Map)

Core Writing Skills Practice

Core skill: Draw evidence from informational texts to support analysis, reflection, and research.
Answer: The student should list the following items: map, black tea, spray bottle, plastic wrap or plastic sheet.

Q1. Give a score of 0, 1, or 2 based on how well the answer meets the criteria listed.
- It should draw a valid conclusion about why steps 1 to 3 should be repeated.
- It should explain that the map would become more stained each time, and that the steps should be repeated until it is the right color.

Q2. Give a score of 0, 1, or 2 based on how well the answer meets the criteria listed.
- It should draw a valid conclusion about why the tea should be allowed to cool down.
- It may refer to how the tea should be cooled to avoid someone being burned, or how boiling tea could ruin the map.

Task 3: Short Story Writing Task

Use the Narrative Writing Rubric to review the work and give a score out of 4.

Task 4: Argument Writing Task

Use the Argument Writing Rubric to review the work and give a score out of 4.

Practice Set 3

Task 1: Short Passage with Questions (Photosynthesis)

Core Writing Skills Practice

Core skill: Use common, grade-appropriate Greek or Latin affixes and roots as clues to the meaning of a word.

Answer: Examples of reasonable definitions are listed below.
chronometer/a device that measures time, biohazard/something harmful to life, polychrome/having many colors, hydrophobia/fear of water

Q1. Give a score of 0, 1, or 2 based on how well the answer meets the criteria listed.
- It should give a definition of the term *photosynthesis*.
- The definition should be in the student's own words.

Q2. Give a score of 0, 1, or 2 based on how well the answer meets the criteria listed.
- The four steps are: 1. Chlorophyll absorbs light energy. 2. Water and carbon dioxide react. 3. Glucose is produced and stored. 4. Oxygen is released.

Task 2: Short Passage with Questions (A Special Student)

Core Writing Skills Practice

Core skill: Write narratives to develop real or imagined experiences or events using effective technique, relevant descriptive details, and well-structured event sequences.

Answer: Use the Narrative Writing Rubric to review the work and give a score out of 4.

Q1. Give a score of 0, 1, or 2 based on how well the answer meets the criteria listed.
- It should make a valid inference about the purpose of not revealing that June is a cow.
- The inference may be that the author wants to make the story interesting, surprise the reader, add humor to the story, or intrigue the reader.

Q2. Give a score of 0, 1, or 2 based on how many valid details are given.
- Valid details include that June eats grass, that June is milked, that June is let out to graze, that June lives in a barn, or that June enjoys being petted.

Q3. Give a score of 0, 1, 2, 3, or 4 based on how well the answer meets the criteria listed.
- It should give an opinion on whether or not June is looked after well.
- It should support the opinion with relevant information from the passage.

Task 3: Long Passage with Essay Question

Use the Informative/Explanatory Writing Rubric to review the work and give a score out of 4.

Task 4: Explanatory Writing Task

Use the Informative/Explanatory Writing Rubric to review the work and give a score out of 4.

Practice Set 4

Task 1: Short Passage with Questions (The Little Things)

Core Writing Skills Practice

Core skill: Write arguments to support claims with clear reasons and relevant evidence.
Answer: The student should give an opinion on whether or not he or she believes that the little things make life great, and should support the opinion with a valid explanation.

Q1. Give a score of 0, 1, or 2 based on how well the answer meets the criteria listed.
- It should identify that the theme is about enjoying your life, looking forward to each day, or appreciating the little things.

Q2. Give a score of 0, 1, or 2 based on how well the answer meets the criteria listed.
- It should explain how the author creates a joyous mood.
- It may refer to how Patrick's actions are described, such as throwing up his arms and jumping out of bed. It may refer to Patrick's dialogue. It may refer to the author's word choice, such as the words "bellow" and "stroll."

Task 2: Short Passage with Questions (Sweet Tooth)

Core Writing Skills Practice

Core skill: Draw evidence from informational texts to support analysis, reflection, and research.
Answer: The student should describe how the paragraph describes events in order or tells how things changed over time.

Q1. Give a score of 0, 1, or 2 based on how many correct ways are listed.
- The ways listed could include that people no longer chew sugarcane raw, that sugar is no longer rare, that sugar is cheaper than it once was, that people now use crystallized sugar, that sugar can now be transported easily, or that sugar is no longer a luxury.

Q2. Give a score of 0, 1, or 2 based on how well the answer meets the criteria listed.
- It should refer to the development that allowed sugarcane juice to be turned into crystallized sugar.
- The conclusion should be supported with details from the passage, such as by describing how crystallized sugar was able to be stored and transported.

Task 3: Argument Writing Task

Use the Argument Writing Rubric to review the work and give a score out of 4.

Task 4: Short Story Writing Task

Use the Narrative Writing Rubric to review the work and give a score out of 4.

Practice Set 5

Task 1: Short Passage with Questions (The Stanley Cup)

Core Writing Skills Practice
Core skill: Write informative/explanatory texts to examine a topic and convey ideas, concepts, and information through the selection, organization, and analysis of relevant content.
Answer: Use the Informative/Explanatory Writing Rubric to give a score out of 4.

Q1. Give a score of 0, 1, or 2 based on how many facts are correctly listed.
- The facts listed could include that it is an ice hockey trophy, that it is awarded to the winner of the National Hockey League championships, that it is the oldest sports trophy in North America, or that it was donated by Lord Stanley of Preston in 1892.

Q2. Give a score of 0, 1, or 2 based on how many opinions are correctly listed.
- The opinions listed could include that it is the most appreciated ice hockey trophy in the world, that being allowed to take possession of the cup makes players appreciate it more, or that people feel honored by having their names engraved on the trophy.

Task 2: Short Passage with Questions (Snowed In)

Core Writing Skills Practice
Core skill: Write narratives to develop real or imagined experiences or events using effective technique, relevant descriptive details, and well-structured event sequences.
Answer: The student should write a paragraph describing the storm from Dr. Nord's point of view.

Q1. Give a score of 0, 1, or 2 based on how well the answer meets the criteria listed.
- The location of the story could be specific, such as the Arctic or Antarctic, or more general, such as in a place with a cold climate. The time of the passage should be winter, and it could be identified as a present or a future setting.

Q2. Give a score of 0, 1, or 2 based on how well the answer meets the criteria listed.
- It may describe details given, such as describing "howling winds.". It may refer to the imagery, such as how the snow "threatened to cover the bunker completely." It may refer to the author's word choice, such as the words "battered," "threatened," or "slam."

Q3. Give a score of 0, 1, 2, 3, or 4 based on how well the answer meets the criteria listed.
- It should make a valid prediction about what will happen next in the passage.
- The prediction should be based on the events of the passage, or information given.

Task 3: Long Passage with Essay Question

Use the Informative/Explanatory Writing Rubric to review the work and give a score out of 4.

Task 4: Explanatory Writing Task

Use the Informative/Explanatory Writing Rubric to review the work and give a score out of 4.

Practice Set 6

Task 1: Short Passage with Questions (Making Money from Junk)

Core Writing Skills Practice

Core skill: Produce clear and coherent writing in which the development, organization, and style are appropriate to task, purpose, and audience.

Answer: The student should create a flyer that persuades people to let you take unwanted items.

Q1. Give a score of 0, 1, or 2 based on how many reasonable problems are listed.
- The problems could include those listed in the passage, which are that you might have to pay to dump waste and that you might sell items for too low a price.
- The problems could include any other reasonable problems that could be predicted, such as being unable to sell the waste, or having too much waste to store.

Q2. Give a score of 0, 1, or 2 based on how well the answer meets the criteria listed.
- It should give an opinion on whether or not the business would be a good one to start, and provide an explanation of why the student has that opinion.

Task 2: Short Passage with Questions (Troy McClure)

Core Writing Skills Practice

Core skill: Conduct short research projects to answer a question, drawing on several sources and generating additional related, focused questions for further research and investigation.

Answer: The correct names are: Homer Simpson/Dan Castellaneta; Marge Simpson/Julie Kavner; Bart Simpson/Nancy Cartwright; and Ned Flanders/Harry Shearer.

Q1. Give a score of 0, 1, or 2 based on how well the table is completed.
- The table could include any of the following four names and details:
  Mike Reiss/He created the character. Troy Donahue/The character was named after him. Doug McClure/The character was named after him. Phil Hartman/He was the voice.

Q2. Give a score of 0, 1, or 2 based on how many opinions are correctly listed.
- The opinions listed could include that it would have been possible to find someone else to be the voice of Troy McClure, that the loss of the character was sad, that the character was much-loved by fans, and that Troy McClure remains one of the show's most popular characters.

Task 3: Short Story Writing Task

Use the Narrative Writing Rubric to review the work and give a score out of 4.

Task 4: Argument Writing Task

Use the Argument Writing Rubric to review the work and give a score out of 4.

Practice Set 7

Task 1: Short Passage with Questions (The Human Skeleton)

Q1. Give a score of 0, 1, or 2 based on how well the answer meets the criteria listed.
- It should relate the information about the purposes of the skeleton to the idea that it is important to look after your bones.
- It should refer to how the bones have many important roles in the body.

Q2. Give a score of 0, 1, or 2 based on how well the answer meets the criteria listed.
- It should draw a reasonable conclusion about the purpose of the section titled "Three Simple Rules."
- It should explain that the purpose of the section is to describe how people can prevent osteoporosis.

Task 2: Short Passage with Questions (Drummer Boy)

Core Writing Skills Practice
Core skill: Draw evidence from literary texts to support analysis, reflection, and research.
Answer: The student should refer to how Tim does not notice what is happening around him or to how he mistakes the silence for the crowd waiting for his solo.

Q1. Give a score of 0, 1, or 2 based on how well the answer meets the criteria listed.
- It should explain that the phrase "nearly jumped out of his chair" shows how startled Tim was by Mr. Paulson. It may also explain that this shows how Tim was lost in his own thoughts.

Q2. Give a score of 0, 1, or 2 based on how well the answer meets the criteria listed.
- It should make a reasonable prediction about how the students in the class felt about Tim's drumming.
- The prediction could be that the students felt annoyed, or that the students were amused by Tim or embarrassed for him.
- It may use details from the passage or the student's personal opinion.

Task 3: Long Passage with Essay Question

Use the Narrative Writing Rubric to review the work and give a score out of 4.

Task 4: Explanatory Writing Task

Use the Informative/Explanatory Writing Rubric to review the work and give a score out of 4.

Practice Set 8

Task 1: Short Passage with Questions (Magnetic North)

Core Writing Skills Practice
Core skill: Draw evidence from informational texts to support analysis, reflection, and research.
Answer: It should describe both the benefits and disadvantages of computerized compasses.

Q1. Give a score of 0, 1, or 2 based on how well the answer meets the criteria listed.
- The student should identify that the author does not support the claim.
- The answer may refer to the lack of evidence or to how the only use mentioned is using compasses for fun during hiking and orienteering activities.

Q2. Give a score of 0, 1, or 2 based on how well the answer meets the criteria listed.
- It should make a reasonable inference about why compasses are less important to sailors than they once were.
- It may describe how new technology has replaced compasses, or how ships use computers and other equipment to navigate.

Task 2: Short Passage with Questions (The Astronomer)

Core Writing Skills Practice
Core skill: Write narratives to develop real or imagined experiences or events using effective technique, relevant descriptive details, and well-structured event sequences.
Answer: Use the Narrative Writing Rubric to review the work and give a score out of 4.

Q1. Give a score of 0, 1, or 2 based on how well the answer meets the criteria listed.
- It should identify that the lesson is about focusing on the here and now, about not being obsessed, or about the dangers of not focusing on what is practical.

Q2. Give a score of 0, 1, or 2 based on how well the answer meets the criteria listed.
- It should identify the personification as being when the stars are described as looking down and laughing at the astronomer.
- It should tell how it shows the astronomer's embarrassment or frustration.

Q3. Give a score of 0, 1, 2, 3, or 4 based on how well the answer meets the criteria listed.
- It should describe how the lesson the astronomer learns is relevant to the student's life.
- It should show insight and the ability to apply the message or general theme to the student's own life.

Task 3: Argument Writing Task

Use the Argument Writing Rubric to review the work and give a score out of 4.

Task 4: Short Story Writing Task

Use the Narrative Writing Rubric to review the work and give a score out of 4.

Practice Set 9

Task 1: Short Passage with Questions (Ruler of Macedon)

Core Writing Skills Practice
Core skill: Write informative/explanatory texts to examine a topic and convey ideas, concepts, and information through the selection, organization, and analysis of relevant content.
Answer: Use the Informative/Explanatory Writing Rubric to give a score out of 4.

Q1. Give a score of 0, 1, or 2 based on how well the answer meets the criteria listed.
- It should give evidence that shows that the author admires Alexander the Great. It may refer to the achievements described in the passage, or the words used to describe Alexander the Great, such as "noteworthy" and "grand."

Q2. Give a score of 0, 1, or 2 based on how many correct achievements are listed.
- The achievements include that he created a very large empire by the age of 30, that he caused the fall of the Persian king Darius III, and that his tactical achievements are still taught today.

Task 2: Short Passage with Questions (The Dwarf Miner)

Core Writing Skills Practice
Core skill: Write narratives to develop real or imagined experiences or events using effective technique, relevant descriptive details, and well-structured event sequences.
Answer: The student should write a paragraph that describes the dwarf being robbed of his gold.

Q1. Give a score of 0, 1, or 2 based on how well the answer meets the criteria listed.
- It should make a reasonable inference about why the dwarf bites the gold.
- It should infer that the dwarf bites the gold to determine that it is real, and refer to what the dwarf says after biting the gold to support the inference.

Q2. Give a score of 0, 1, or 2 based on how well the answer meets the criteria listed.
- It should summarize the main events of the passage.
- The main events should include that the dwarf started mining gold, collected a bowl of gold nuggets, and then left for home.

Task 3: Long Passage with Essay Question

Use the Informative/Explanatory Writing Rubric to review the work and give a score out of 4.

Task 4: Personal Narrative Writing Task

Use the Narrative Writing Rubric to review the work and give a score out of 4.

Practice Set 10

Task 1: Short Passage with Questions (The Park)

Core Writing Skills Practice

Core skill: Write informative/explanatory texts to examine a topic and convey ideas, concepts, and information through the selection, organization, and analysis of relevant content.

Answer: The student should write a paragraph describing a place that he or she enjoys spending time. Students should explain why they enjoy spending time in that place.

Q1. Give a score of 0, 1, or 2 based on how well the answer meets the criteria listed.
- It should circle one of the words. Any of the words could be reasonable answers, as long as the choice is supported.
- It should include a well-supported explanation of why the student chose that word.

Q2. Give a score of 0, 1, or 2 based on how many things are correctly listed.
- The things she saw people doing could include having picnics, rowing boats on the lake, feeding bread to the ducks, or pretending to be a statue.

Task 2: Short Passage with Questions (The Desert Oasis)

Core Writing Skills Practice

Core skill: Write narratives to develop real or imagined experiences or events using effective technique, relevant descriptive details, and well-structured event sequences.

Answer: The student should use sensory details to describe a hot desert.

Q1. Give a score of 0, 1, or 2 based on how well the answer meets the criteria listed.
- It should describe how the author creates a sense of hopelessness.
- It may refer to the description of Serian's actions, the author's word choice, or to the tone.

Q2. Give a score of 0, 1, or 2 based on how well the answer meets the criteria listed.
- It should make a reasonable prediction about what happens next.
- The prediction could describe what Serian does when he arrives at the oasis, or could describe Serian realizing that the oasis is not real.

Q3. Give a score of 0, 1, 2, 3, or 4 based on how well the answer meets the criteria listed.
- It should describe how Serian feels tired, exhausted, or hopeless at the start.
- It should describe how Serian feels relieved, excited, or overjoyed after he sees the oasis.

Task 3: Short Story Writing Task

Use the Narrative Writing Rubric to review the work and give a score out of 4.

Task 4: Argument Writing Task

Use the Argument Writing Rubric to review the work and give a score out of 4.

INFORMATIVE/EXPLANATORY WRITING RUBRIC

This writing rubric is based on the state standards and describes the features that are expected in student writing. Give students a score out of 4 based on how well the answer meets the criteria. Then average the scores to give a total score out of 4. Students can also be given feedback and guidance based on the criteria below.

	Score	Notes
Organization and Purpose To receive a full score, the response will: • have an opening that introduces the topic • have a clear focus • be well-organized with related information grouped together • use formatting (e.g. headings) and graphics (e.g. charts, diagrams) when appropriate • provide a concluding statement or section		
Evidence and Elaboration To receive a full score, the response will: • develop the topic with facts, details, quotations, or examples • include relevant text-based evidence when appropriate		
Written Expression To receive a full score, the response will: • be clear and easy to understand • have good transitions between ideas • use language to communicate ideas effectively • have an appropriate style		
Writing Conventions To receive a full score, the response will: • have few or no spelling errors • have few or no grammar errors • have few or no capitalization errors • have few or no punctuation errors		
Total Score		

ARGUMENT WRITING RUBRIC

This writing rubric is based on the state standards and describes the features that are expected in student writing. Give students a score out of 4 based on how well the answer meets the criteria. Then average the scores to give a total score out of 4. Students can also be given feedback and guidance based on the criteria below.

	Score	Notes
Organization and Purpose To receive a full score, the response will: • have an opening that introduces the topic and states the claim • have a clear focus • be well-organized with related information grouped together • provide a concluding statement or section		
Evidence and Elaboration To receive a full score, the response will: • express clear reasons to support the claim • include evidence to support the claim • include relevant text-based evidence when appropriate		
Written Expression To receive a full score, the response will: • be clear and easy to understand • have good transitions between ideas • use language to communicate ideas effectively • have an appropriate style		
Writing Conventions To receive a full score, the response will: • have few or no spelling errors • have few or no grammar errors • have few or no capitalization errors • have few or no punctuation errors		
Total Score		

NARRATIVE WRITING RUBRIC

This writing rubric is based on the state standards and describes the features that are expected in student writing. Give students a score out of 4 based on how well the answer meets the criteria. Then average the scores to give a total score out of 4. Students can also be given feedback and guidance based on the criteria below.

	Score	Notes
Organization and Purpose To receive a full score, the response will: • have an effective opening that introduces the situation, characters, or event • have a logical and organized event sequence • have an effective ending		
Development and Elaboration To receive a full score, the response will: • have clearly developed characters, setting, and events • use narrative techniques such as dialogue and pacing effectively • use precise words and phrases • use relevant descriptive details • use sensory language		
Written Expression To receive a full score, the response will: • be clear and easy to understand • have good transitions between ideas • use language to communicate ideas effectively		
Writing Conventions To receive a full score, the response will: • have few or no spelling errors • have few or no grammar errors • have few or no capitalization errors • have few or no punctuation errors		
Total Score		

Made in the USA
Monee, IL
25 January 2022